S0-ADA-924

THE STORY OF COMOCK THE ESKIMO

as told to Robert Flaherty/edited by Edmund Carpenter

SIMON & SCHUSTER · NEW YORK

All rights reserved
including the right of reproduction
in whole or in part in any form
Copyright © 1968 by Edmund Carpenter
Published by Simon & Schuster, Inc., Children's Book Division
Rockefeller Center, 630 Fifth Avenue
New York, New York 10020
Drawings from the collection of the Royal
Ontario Museum appear here by permission.

Second Printing

SBN 671-65034-3 Trade
SBN 671-65035-1 Library
Designed by Eve Metz
Library of Congress Catalog Card Number: 68-29757
Manufactured in the United States of America
Printed by Sanders Printing Corp., New York
Bound by Economy Bookbinding Corp., New Jersey

This book didn't just happen. Its parts belong together.

I heard Robert Flaherty tell Comock's story during the winter of 1949–50, over the BBC. It seemed to me then that this account — of human life reduced to a man, a woman, fire-making stones, and the will to perpetuate life — was ultimately an account of the rebirth of mankind.

That summer I visited the island in Hudson Bay where Comock probably lived during the ten years of this story. On an adjoining island I came upon the grave of an unknown whaler who, like Comock, had struggled to stay alive on a deserted arctic island. Later I heard from a retired fur trader the details of this tragedy.

Not long after that trip I discovered an almost-unknown publication: Drawings by Enooesweetok of the Sikosilingmint Tribe, Fox Land, Baffin Island, *Robert Flaherty, privately printed, Toronto, 1915. It was a folio of twenty-one exquisite sketches made in 1913–14. Flaherty died in 1951, so I asked Frances Flaherty, his widow, to see if she could find the originals. She found two of these, plus nineteen unpublished ones. She also found a notebook containing sketches by another Eskimo, including the sketch opposite, which shows Flaherty in three different acts of filming — directing, setting up, and shooting — all shown simultaneously. These drawings are now in the Royal Ontario Museum.*

At that time, I had an office in the Royal Ontario Museum, whose collections included Eskimo tools and carvings gathered by Flaherty between 1910 and 1914. Some of these may have been made by Comock during his years of isolation, and so I have included sketches of a few in this book.

I have reassembled these scattered parts here so that others may know this story as I have known it. In the eighteen years since I first heard it, it has often been in my thoughts and will not go out of mind and be forgotten.

— Edmund Carpenter

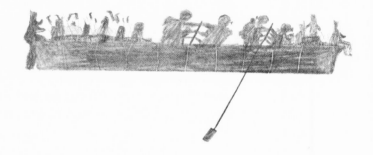

In the year 1912 I was in a little Hudson's Bay Company post at Cape Wolstenholme, the northeast extreme of Hudson Bay. Over breakfast one morning the manager of the post said, "How about some hunting? We'll take the sloop and sail around the nose of Cape Wolstenholme. We might see something in the way of game. A walrus, perhaps, or possibly a bear among the cliffs."

We started. We came to a ledge jutting off from the cliff face, landed upon it and, climbing up some fifty feet, sat down. I was looking through my glass at thousands of little specks, sea pigeons flying among the rocks of a nearby island. Suddenly on the water before the island I saw a small boat rowing toward us. It sprawled clumsily over the lumpy sea. It drew nearer. Its occupants were Eskimos. A man was steering at the stern, two others were at the oars. It drew nearer, close in. It was almost a third as broad as it was long, which was not more than fifteen feet, but within it we counted thirteen people, grown-ups and children, huddled together, and among them two dogs as well. Over the children and the dogs a woman held a stick to hit them if by moving suddenly they should threaten the balance of the cockleshell. Why the amazing craft did not capsize we could not understand, until I saw its waterline, a series of inflated seal bladders tied at intervals around it. They alone kept the craft afloat. The Eskimos, their dogs — as wild as wolves — cowering between their legs, stared at us out of their twinkling slant-eyes. They looked like something half bird and half man, for their costumes were not made of the usual deerskin or bearskin or hairy seal, but of the skins of the ivory duck, feathers and all, sewn together. They were not afraid. The mother's babe that she carried naked in the hood of her *koolitah* [parka] suddenly crawled halfway out along her bare shoulder, looked up at us for a few moments with big brown eyes, then stuck out its tiny arm and smiled. That broke the ice. I took its hand, it smiled again, the mother smiled and then the father, one of the finest looking Eskimos I have ever seen. He had a long, finely chiseled nose, a chin as solid as a rock and penetrating, far-seeing eyes. His hair hung to his shoulders. "*Chimo* [hi!]," he said.

"Chimo," echoed his wife.

"Chimo," piped the children. The mother twitched her shoulder on which the baby lay; it understood and smiled again.

"Who are you?" I asked.

"My name is Comock," he answered, smiling expectantly.

"Where in the world have you come from?"

"From far away, from big island, from far over there," he answered, pointing out to the west. "You see, our *umiak* [boat] is not very good," and he laughed and his family laughed with him. We took them all aboard and, with this incredible contraption in tow, sailed on back toward the post. He told me this story.

— Robert Flaherty

COMOCK'S STORY

For ten winters and ten summers we had been living on an island, far out on the sea (said Comock). See, my wife has kept count. She has written it here on the handle of my harpoon. (And he showed me the harpoon, the wooden handle of which was notched from end to end, a notch for each moon.)

The land where we used to live was poor; no walrus, few seals, no deer. I had two wives and many children. I did not know anymore how to keep them alive, but I had an idea. I'd had it for a long time. Far out at sea from my land there is an island. None of my people had ever seen it, it was so far away. I heard about it from the White Chief of a whaler. He told me there were days when the sky over it was almost black with the flight of birds, the big birds that honk, and there were many lakes and ponds, the Chief of the big whaler said, and around them the big birds brought up their young. There were many foxes, there were many deer and there were many bear and schools of walrus on the little islands along the coast, and seals — many, many seals.

And they'd be so easy to hunt, the Chief of the whaler said, because no Eskimo lived on all that land. Never had he seen such game as was on this island. He told me if I could get out to it I would never be hungry. I could not keep from thinking of that land; I talked about it over and over with my wives. There was only one way to go, we all agreed — by sled over the ice fields in winter, in the moon of the most cold when there is the least chance of the ice field parting and drifting off.

"Two days sledding," I told my family. "Two long days it will take us if our dogs are strong and we are strong, and there is not too much rough ice."

"*Ae* [yes]," my wife said, "the rough ice will be the worst." You see, we could be caught and travel no farther in one sun than a seal might swim from one breathing hole to another. Winter came on; we had little food. More than most winters it was poor; no deer upon the land, no walrus at the ice edge and the seals — not many.

"We will go," said my wife.

"Yes, we will go," said my sons.

And there was another, Annunglung, who sailed with me. He was not a good hunter; he had only one wife, but he was not afraid. "Yes," he said, "I will go too." And so said his wife.

The sun got lower every day. We watched the ice from the high cliffs that lean out over the sea. Day by day we watched that ice. On the days when we had to go hunting one of the women watched it for us. The ice grew fast, for it was cold, until at last nowhere was there water, and the big smokes of the freezing were gone — the ice was everywhere. "Now is the time, now we will go. *Twavee* [quick]!" I said.

"Twavee!" said everyone. We could hardly hear the howling of our dogs. We had three sleds of dogs, twelve dogs to each sled. They were good dogs. We had taken care to feed them well, and now they howled to be off.

In the beginning the ice was rough for the first big wind of the winter had jammed the ice hard against the coast and piled it up to many times the height I stand. It was heavy going, but at last we worked out of it without hurting our sleds and we got smooth ice. We traveled fast on this smooth ice for the wind had packed the snow hard, and our feet did not sink and the dogs' feet moved so fast my eyes would swim to look at them. We never had so little use for the long whip — their tails never fell, their traces never touched the snow. We only rested twice — to untangle the traces and to clear the ice from between the toes of the dogs' feet. There was good hunting too — my leader dog was always turning his head, so many were the breathing holes of the seal — but "We must not stop," I said.

"We must not stop," said my wife, "ae," and everyone agreed.

At last the long shadows in the snow grew blue like the sky. The shining left the edges of the ice and the long shadows drew away like the edge of an ice field moving slowly out from the land. Still the traces of the dogs did not touch the ground. There was not much light from the stars, and we stumbled.

When the moon did rise it was only half a moon. It did not give us much light, and we stumbled, and there were wails from the dogs and that was because we were now truly tired and it took much shaking to keep our children awake. "*Tiamak*" [here – now; that's it], I said. "We will stop."

"Ae," said everyone. And the dogs sank into the snow, too tired to fight, and they buried their noses between their paws and let the snow-smoke drift over them, and while our women sat in the shelter of our sleds and nursed the small children, Annunglung and I went off with our snow knives and harpoons, and by good luck we found along a crack in the ice a deep drift of snow. We cut out a block of snow. The edges cut sharp and did not crumble and then we cut out block after block and built our igloo.

The dogs between sleep kept watching us and when we had built our igloo
and from the inside cut out the door and crawled out, they were all around
us howling for their seal. I had to use my long whip to keep them away, and
then our wives crept inside and they were all smiling for they were away
from the burn of the cold, and they lit our seal-oil lamps and put our willow
mats and deerskins down while the children chewed their pieces of raw
seal. Outside we gave our dogs their meat, and then they bedded
themselves in the snow in the shelter of the sleds and the igloo, and let
the snow cover them again. Annunglung and I went inside, and our wives cut
seal meat and filled our mouths, and we said the night was full of good
signs, though there were growls now and then running through the ice,
growing louder and louder as they came toward us, and sounding in our
ears like Nanook the bear rushing toward the spear, but I said, "Never
mind, there is always growling from the sea." So we fell asleep, cold though
our igloo was, as a new igloo always is when there is no wind.

When I awakened I was happy, for our ice window was blue, and by that I knew that there was no snow-smoke in the air. My head wife made fire in her willow down, and she blew it into a flame and lit the lamp. "Look at our children, Comock," she said, "they are warm." There were little smokes rising from the deerskin robes under which they slept.

We were out early. There was still fire in the stars. It was so cold that the spit from our mouths froze before it struck the ground. We were out on the ice so far now that looking backward I could not see land, and besides there was rough ice — much rough ice. I climbed up on one high piece, and looking ahead all I could see was rough ice. We moved very slowly, up and down, up and down — the smallest child who walks could keep up with us. Many times this rough ice would tangle the long traces of the dogs and it was hard to keep them from laming or wounding one another, for all this tangling gave them the madness to kill.

Not until the sun was high could we get out of this rough ice, and though it was cold our bodies were wet with sweat, and the muzzles of the dogs were white, and they were quick with their breathing and wanted to lie down. "But we must keep on," I said. "Look — I do not like the sky."

"No, we do not like the sky," said everyone. There were clouds in it, and they began to cross the sun and there was more and more wind, and everywhere over the ice the smoke of the snow was rising.

We kept on and we went fast for a while, and then we struck young ice. And then we had to go faster still, for it would bend with our weight — if we

stopped we would have broken through. From this young ice we struck old
ice once more, and it was smooth and again we traveled fast, though the
wind was still stronger and the smoke of the snow was thick in the air.

The wind was growing stronger and there was no blue left in the sky, and
all three sleds had to keep close together or we might lose one another.

I did not like this wind. It might part the ice, for it blew off the land, but we
all laughed and said it was a little matter, there was no harm in that wind.
Darkness came early, so filled was the sky with the flying snow, and we were
tired, and we stumbled. "It is enough," I said.

"Ae," said my wife.

"Ae," said everyone, and the dogs sank in the snow.

Though our igloo walls were thick, and we could hear the wind, after we
finished eating the red meat and lay down to sleep, we could hear it more.
We wondered how far we were still from the big island.

"It is strange that with all this wind we can hear no growling in the sea —
the ice now must be very strong," I said.

But someone else said, "Even if the ice is strong there still could be
growling of the sea." We did not talk another word for sleep was heavy in
our eyes.

I slept near the door so that I could be the first out in the morning. I was deep in sleep. Then I awoke — why I do not know. I could hear the fierce roaring of the wind. But even now though I listened hard I could hear no growling from the sea. Then I wondered why I had wakened — fool, I called myself. I looked at Annunglung and his wife and his children asleep. I was trimming the moss wicks of our seal-oil lamp before lying down again, and then I heard it. Far out at first, then quick like the wind it began coming toward me — one long, louder and louder roar! And now under me I could feel trembling. I knew what it was. It was the ice, it was parting, and it cut our igloo in two. The lamp fell; there was no light. "Hold on to each other!" I yelled to everyone in the darkness. "Hold on to each other or we are lost!" The dogs were howling, the children crying, and there were screams from our wives. I could not see it, but open water was at our feet. "Hold together!" I yelled. I could not hear. "Are we all together?" I cried.

"No, we are not together, we are not together!" It was my head wife. "Don't you hear, don't you hear?" she was shrieking.

"Stop," I cried, "then I shall hear." Even so they were already far — I could barely hear them — my young wife, Annunglung's wife, one of his and two of my young children and my second oldest son. Then their calling died away. We called — we listened — we called again, but we could only hear the roaring of the storm and the growling of the sea.

It was black with darkness, and I had to walk from one to another feeling their hands. We stumbled in our walking and fell down, but we held our hands and we got into the hollow of some big blocks of ice. We stood there until the light came into the sky and then we tried to see across the open water which was not far, but we could not see well, for it was covered with its own thick smoking from the cold. I was glad we could not see, for we could do nothing even if we did see our people and my wife still had her fits of screaming.

I went off to see the place where our igloo had been standing but there was only the smoke and water of the sea. Everything — all but one sled — was gone. All that we owned was gone — the willow mats, the deerskins, the stone pots, the stone lamp for our snow melting, all my knives, spears, harpoons — everything gone. Then a thought struck me and I was truly frightened and I walked fast and I called out to my wife as I walked, "The stones, the stones — have you got them?"

"The stones, did you say?" asked my wife, and she stood still and she looked frightened.

"Yes," I said, "the stones, have you got them?" Then quickly her hands went to the pouch in her koolitah. And for a long time she was feeling. And then at last, "Yes, Comock," she said, "I've got them." They were the stones we must have to make the sparks for our fires.

Then I said to my wife, "There surely will not be time for grieving now. Everything is gone. We have only one sled, my ivory knife with which to cut the snow blocks for our igloo building and your stones for fire-making."

My wife said, "It is well, Comock, we have something."

"Yes," I said, "but no spears, no harpoons — we cannot kill bear — we cannot kill seal."

"There are the dogs," my wife said, "and there are the harnesses of the dogs that are gone. We can eat them," my wife said.

"No," said my eldest son, "we cannot eat the harnesses. The harnesses they are gone. They were tied to the lost sleds."

"Well, anyway, there are the dogs," my wife said.

"Ae," I said, "there are the dogs."

"Ae," said everyone.

For one moon we were on the broken ice, drifting — we drifted one way many days — we drifted another way many days. It made us feel small to drift in this foolish way upon the sea.

We shared with our dogs the dog meat upon which we lived. "The meat of the dogs does not keep one warm like the meat of the seal," someone said.

"Yes, and our dogs are no longer warm," someone said.

And then someone else said, "They will bear watching, what with all the children and we with no spears to kill."

"I will make clubs," I said. "There are a few crosspieces of the sled that can be spared, and they will make clubs."

And we took the crosspieces off our sleds and they made clubs. Besides these crosspieces, I had my long whip — I could kill ptarmigan with it, and if I had to, I could split a dog's ear in two.

"But the crosspieces and whip are not enough," said my wife. "There are some dogs we will have to tie up. The dogs upon which we live are the weaker dogs — the dangerous ones are those that are strong."

"We must have patience with the dogs," I said, "even if they try to kill, for we will need our dogs even more than fire if we ever come upon land again."

"Yes," said my wife, "but what of the children, Comock? If they should stumble — I get sick from watching."

There was much hunting to find good stones. We searched far though we were all weak. Not in one day did we find the good stones, but we found them just the same. My young sons found a piece of driftwood buried in the snow. I made a knife and a spearhead of the stones, and we cut the driftwood, and at last we made a harpoon. Everyone laughed and said they had seen better harpoons. That night when we all lay down to sleep, someone said, "It will be good when we get seal."

And then someone said, "Yes, it will be good when we get oil."

"Yes," said someone, "it is the oil we need most. Hunger is one thing, but these nights of darkness are the worst." We went to sleep.

There was another storm and for a long time we could not see. But when the smoke of the snow cleared from the sky we saw the edge of our ice breaking high upon something. It was land. This land was low like the sea, but we knew it was land because we could see black specks in the whiteness and those black specks in the whiteness were rocks sticking up through the snow. "This must be the big island," said my wife.

"Yes," I said.

When we got to this land we built an igloo, and in the darkness, for we had no lamp, we lay down to sleep. "It is funny," said someone, "the land is so still." For a long time we could not sleep because the land was so still.

With the daylight coming I took my leader dog to find me a breathing hole of the seal, and not far out on the ice he stopped and he smelled a hole. And there I waited all day until the seal had made his rounds of his breathing holes, and at last the bubbles of his breathing began to rise in my hole, and I took up my harpoon and killed the seal.

There was darkness in the igloo when I clubbed my way against the dogs through the long tunnel dragging my seal. Everyone made noise, and the dogs in the tunnel made much noise. And there was talking and laughing, and my wife soon got oil and from her stones struck fire, and there was light in our igloo, and everyone smiling could see one another. The seal which lay before us was a big seal, and we fed our dogs, and we kept on eating and sleeping and eating. It was all mixed up together.

We made more knives and better knives, and we made more harpoons. And on all these days there were seals. "The dogs do not show their ribs now," said my wife. "And did you ever see such strong children? But we soon must get skins for new clothing. Are there deer on this island?"

"We will find out," I said, "if there are deer on this island."

"It will be good to have soft deerskins for clothing," said my wife.

"Which way shall we go? To the north or to the south?" For a long time we did not know, and then my wife said, "I have a feeling — let us go north."

"Ae, said everyone, "let us go north."

We were many days traveling for there was much hunting. All the way there were bear and there were seal and there were walrus, and at last we saw deer. And we made our kill, and my wife got the skins for our clothing.

The days now were all light. The ice was scattering on the sea, and the warm sun bared the ground, and the big birds that honk came up from the south and they nested round the edges of the lakes and ponds. Everywhere were these big birds and their crying and their flying filled the sky, but in time they lost the feathers of their wings. Then we ran after them and ran them down.

From driftwood and sealskins we made a kayak and I hunted the little
islands off the shore, and on some there were walrus. From the tusks of the
walrus we got the ivory for our sled runners, ivory for our snow knives,
ivory for our harpoons, and ivory for needles for my wife.

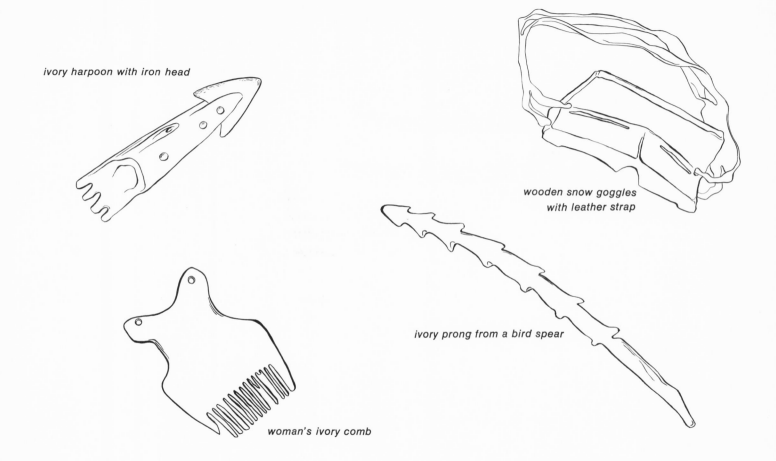

ivory harpoon with iron head

wooden snow goggles
with leather strap

ivory prong from a bird spear

woman's ivory comb

There were bear. We made trips over the land far in from the sea, and in one camp, where we fished salmon from the stream, the bear were so many that I had to tie bones together on a string so that in the wind they would knock and make noise and so keep the bear away while we had our sleep.

During the warmest days of the summer we were camped along a shore where there was a river in which many salmon were swimming. We had just finished with our day's fishing when our children came running to us over the sand. Their eyes were big and they were saying, "We have seen something strange, a monster which has come up from the sea and it is now lying on the shore." We all went to where they said the monster was. Soon we came to a point. It lay behind that point, they said. We walked carefully to the point and we looked over the point, and then we saw it. Its black holes looked like eyes. It had been shoved far up from the water by the ice. It was very old, I could see by the moss and the whiteness of its wood. My wife did not like to go near.

"Something might come out of the holes," she said.

"Don't be foolish," I said, but she hung behind. With Annunglung and my sons I climbed up on it, and the first thing we found was iron, good iron, not only gray iron, but yellow iron and the red iron which is softer than the yellow iron. And these two, when we rubbed them, gleamed in the sun. And all of that ship was good wood. Some of this good wood was hard like stone, and there was enough of it to make the runners for sleds and handles for spears and harpoons for ten times more people than there are fingers on my hands. "Come," I yelled to my wife. "Come," I said, "you will not believe your eyes."

But she said, "No, something might come out of the holes."

We found pots for my wife, pots of gray iron, pots of red iron, pots of yellow iron, and, the best of all, we found axes and knives, knives for my wife for the cutting of meat, knives for the cutting of skins, knives that were big and knives that were small and knives for the cutting of wood, big knives as long as my arm, and we ground them and ground them with stones until blood came to our fingers we ground them so sharp.

But for all this treasure my foolish wife was too frightened to go near the ship, and my children would only peep at it from behind big rocks. They could see them, they said, the ghosts of white men going in and coming out of the holes. But I used to go and my sons used to go and we found many things, and a glass that could see was one of the things. "Ae," said my wife when I gave it to her, "there are truly good things that come out of the black holes of the ghosts."

"Yes," I said, "but even ghosts will do you no harm, no more than the ghost of your face in the glass."

"Maybe you're right, Comock," she said, and she looked and she smiled at the ghost of her face in the glass.

"We are rich," I said. We were all sitting on the sand around a big driftwood fire.

"Yes," said my wife, "we are rich, but if only the rest of the people were with us, they would have everything too. We could all be happy together."

"We can't have everything," I said. "No one has everything."

"It is true," said Annunglung. "No matter how much we have, there is always more that we are wanting."

"But if only I could have those that went off in the ice," said my wife. "When the storms come across from our land I cannot keep their calling out of my ears, and dead they may be, but they are still on the ice. I am sure that I can hear them."

Our second winter on the island was a good winter. We were happy, even my wife. But as the winter drew on she talked more of our old land, much hunger she had for our old land and for our people who had been lost on the ice of the sea. "Maybe they landed on our old land," she said, "maybe their ice came back again and they landed there, after all, who can tell?" she said.

"It is foolish your talk," I said. "You have forgotten all that hunger we had in our old land, and if you have not forgotten that hunger, have you forgotten the ice that lies between? That ice," I said — "for myself I would rather trust a hungry dog."

"Maybe you are right, Comock," she said.

The oldest of my sons was growing big. He was almost a man and he was learning fast in his kayak and learning fast with his sled and he was good at his hunting — he had already killed his first deer.

One night — it was winter again — he had been away two days with Annunglung on the ice out at sea. He came into our igloo with the children laughing and screaming and helping him drag in his first seal — not a small seal, but a big square-flipper seal. We could not believe he could kill such a big seal.

"Yes," said Annunglung, "there was much fighting, but he killed him — I sat over one breathing hole and he sat over another, and when the seal came to his hole he stood up and struck down with his harpoon. The seal sounded and dived, so fast with his line he was pulled to the ice, so hard I thought surely some of his bones were broken. But he had the end of his line wrapped around him where he lay over the hole. I got him to his feet, but he was pulled down again and again. At last he was mostly on his feet, and he pulled in some of his line, and he pulled in more of his line and then more of his line and then it came easy, and at last the seal was dead."

My son said that anyone could have killed such a seal — a child could have killed almost such a seal. But my wife said, "Lie down beside it; it's longer than you."

But my son said, "My dogs, they are hungry," and he crawled out of the tunnel with all the children behind him.

My wife turned to me and said, "Comock, our son is now a hunter."

"No," I said, "but maybe he will be before the end of this winter — there is still his first walrus and there is still his first bear."

During the moon of the shortest days a big storm blowing again from our old land drove in big fields of ice and piled it high along the shores. At sea there was no open water for a long time, and that was the end of our good hunting. For many days I was hunting with my sons on the ice for seals, but all that we got was hardly enough to keep us alive. In these days Annunglung began to stay at home — something had come over him. Annunglung was always a silent man, never speaking much, not even of his lost wife and his lost children; but now, said my wife, he would sit in the igloo all day, just looking. This went on for days. We would come home perhaps with a seal, and Annunglung would say, "It's a poor man, Comock, who shares your igloo and eats your seal and does not do his share of hunting."

And then I would say, "Why do you not come out with us hunting?" And for a long time we would be silent though all our eyes would be upon him and waiting to hear what he would say. But it would be as if his mouth had been frozen — he would not move it again.

This would happen many times, and when we came home there would be Annunglung sitting in the igloo and my wife would say, "He has not moved all day long."

One night we came home with two big seals — we had been away two days — and there was Annunglung sitting and saying nothing, and I saw by my wife's face that she was frightened. My wife took me into the tunnel to be away from his hearing, and my wife made her voice very small and she said, "Comock, you must not leave me and my young children here alone again — I am frightened. Have you seen his eyes?"

"No," I said.

"You must see his eyes," she said.

As soon as the dogs were fed, my eldest son fastened the snow-block door for the night. And then we gathered around our seal and sat down to our eating, and we could not help looking at Annunglung who did not sit with us but sat near the lamp, not even eating the seal meat we had put into his hand. My wife, who sat near me, kept touching my arm. "Annunglung, are you not hungry?" I asked, hoping he would look up in the way that there would be light in his eyes. He looked and the light of the lamp was in his eyes, and then the meat in my mouth stood still, and truly I was frightened — the little black balls of his eyes — they had grown so small.

Then I told my sons to go alone to the hunt. I found and hid Annunglung's spears and harpoons. His knives, my wife said, he always kept under his sleeping mat. I found them and hid them too. There were many days of storms. My sons brought home no seals. We grew hungry. "Let our sons stay at home," my wife said. "You go for a seal this time, for we must soon have seals." I went out on the ice and stayed away two days, but the storms were too heavy. I could do no hunting. I had to come home. The night was half done when I did come home, and late though it was there was still a bright light shining through the ice window. Then I knew something was wrong. When I crawled into my igloo my wife was sitting up and not moving and there was fright on her face, and my sons were sitting up, and they were frightened too. Annunglung was sitting like a stone, not moving and not talking, but there was something in his eyes that told me that three men would not be so strong.

We took turns sitting and watching all that night and all the next day, and
I tried to think what I would have to do. "Maybe he will get well," said my
wife. And sometimes it looked as if this would be so, for in these times he
would sleep a little, and he would eat a little, but I knew in the end that he
would never be well. And truly this was so, for there were now deep lines
on his face, and his teeth were set hard and sometimes they ground. And
there was blood from his tongue, and in his eyes there was that shine and
the black balls of them were truly very small.

We were hungry and my dogs were hungry — they were all ribs and there
was whiteness on their mouths. We had one family of young dogs — those
the dogs had already killed and eaten. And there was Annunglung, more
and more still, and there was more and more hunger and my wife said,
"Soon, Comock, you must kill some seals."

Then there was a night, and on this night everyone was asleep. And I who was watching was almost asleep, and then I heard a noise. It was Annunglung. I looked. He could not see my half-open eyes. He got up and he looked — he looked toward me a long time, then he looked at my sons a long time, and then he looked at my wife and my children, and then he looked all over the igloo and then he looked under his mat and there was no knife, and then he looked around again, and at last with no noise he began to crawl out through the tunnel of the igloo. This tunnel was narrow — he could not quickly turn. I followed him. I came upon him as he reached the end of the tunnel and stood up to get a knife and spear. Then he heard me, but I struck. Then he struck. Then I was glad, and if it had not been so I would not be alive. It was his blood the dogs smelled first.

When I came into the igloo again, no one had heard the fight or the fighting of the dogs. They were still asleep.

There was no more want that winter, or the next winter or the next winter. Our children were growing. One daughter was almost a woman. "It is well," my wife said, for it was more than she could do to take care of my kills and our son's kills and sew the skins for our boots and clothing.

Then the day came when my son all alone speared his first bear. My wife said, "Our son now is a man, Comock."

"Ae," I said, he is now a man." But my wife still kept on with her talking as a woman will.

"Does it mean nothing to you, Comock, now that he is a man?"

"What do you mean?" I asked her.

But she said, "How can we go on living on this big island, and no wife for our son who is now a man? Besides," she said, "our other sons, too. They will all soon kill their first bear. We are only one family on all this big island, Comock," she said. "We will have to go sometime — if we don't we will die out on this big island, for all of its deer and all of its bear and all of its walrus and the bones of the white man's ship from which we get the good wood and the good iron for our knives and our harpoons. Besides, there's the ghost of Annunglung, Comock. We must leave this big island."

"The ghost of Annunglung," I said, "will come to us wherever we are. We must stay, we are fools to trust the sea — if we do, maybe we will die," I said.

"Maybe," said my wife, "but here it is sure — longer maybe, but sure."

"But I am afraid of the ice that lies between this big island and our old land," I would say, "and it will break on our crossing."

"The break of the ice on our crossing will not be so bad as if we stay here," was always my wife's answer. To this no words would come to my mouth.

Now came days that were still — there were no more big smokes rising
from the sea, and these days were the days of the most cold. The nights of
these days were the nights of the Big Lights, and these Big Lights were the
red of pale meat and like the warm coat of the bear and like the weed of
the sea. And sometimes the Big Lights were so strong the moon was the
green of clear ice, and all the snow on the land was the green of clear ice.
And these Big Lights would move slowly like the long waves on the sea, or
they would turn, or they would jump, for they were never still. And my wife
said these Big Lights were truly the spirits of unborn children playing in the
sky, and she said for many days they may be playing in the sky, and now,
she said, it was the time we should be crossing the big ice on the sea.

She said this many times and at last I said, "Maybe you are right — if ever we go, now is the time. In all our ten winters on this big island never have there been such good signs, such stillness on the sea or so much of the Big Light playing in the sky. We will go," I said. "Tiamak, to this big island."

"Ae," she said.

"Ae," said everyone.

There were yet some stars when we started. The air was still. "Twavee," I said.

"Twavee," said everyone. We had strong dogs, two sleds, twelve dogs to each sled. All day we traveled over the sea. We did not stop for seal and we did not stop for bear. There was much smooth ice and there was bad ice, but mostly the ice was smooth. We never traveled so fast over the ice of the sea.

On the next day it was the same, it was wonderful how fast we were going. On the third day we saw the land. We got close in, and the land we saw was our own land — the land which leans over the sea.

But now the ice was rough and piled higher than any I'd ever seen; from one high place one sled fell, and it fell so hard it broke in two. We had to leave this sled where it was and its load of good deerskins and good pots and the whole of one seal. We kept on, it was a long time, but at last we got close to the land which leans over the sea, and we could see, high up, its caves and dark places, but we had to lift our heads to look up at its edge, it rose so high in the sky.

We had to stop. We were tired — too tired to go on. From the dogs there was quick breathing and there was foam on their mouths. While we got rest and slow breathing, I wondered how ever we could get into the big land which was now almost leaning over us as well as the sea.

We were deep in one place in this big ice, and the dogs, their traces all tangled, were all thrown together like fish in a net, and they were fighting to kill. We were trying to stop them and then with my feet I felt something. It was the ice — it was moving. My wife and my children were on a high ledge behind us, and though I could not hear them above the great noise of the dogs, I could see them waving their arms. At first it looked as if it was the big land that moved, passing us by. "Twavee," I yelled, "twavee." We must go back — we must go back out of this rough ice. We threw away half the load of the sled, and we turned and we began to work back. And it took all day to get onto the smooth ice, and all the time the ice field we were on was drifting. By nightfall it looked small, the land which leans over the sea.

We got rest and we started again, but soon we could hardly move, so deep were we in the ice. We looked small, like children. To climb some of the big pieces we had to cut footholds with our knives and then from the top pull up our dogs by their traces and then lower them down over the sides and then by the master lines pull up the sleds and then lower them down over the sides.

For a long time, two moons, we drifted. And then one morning again we saw land, the big land on one side, but nearer to us still an island which rose high, almost straight up from the sea.

Our ice closed on this island like a big hand on a throat, and after the ice had done with its piling and breaking and rafting we climbed and we crawled through it, and got on to the shore, and climbed its big cliffs and on the top made our camp. Here we lived for the rest of the winter and through the spring and through the summer. And there were the eggs of eider ducks to eat and the skin of eider ducks for clothes, and there were sea pigeons which we caught in the cliffs and there were seals sometimes as well.

In these days we were much troubled for we did not know how we could get off this island, for between us and the big land, though it was not far, there was always the tide that runs swift like a river. And always, if there is ice in it, it is not ice we could cross, for it is the ice that is loose and the ice that is wild, always turning and tumbling and going up and down.

"If there were no ice and we had an umiak," I said, "then we might cross."

"Yes," said someone, and there was much laughing. "If our legs were long enough we could walk through the sea."

"Yes, but just the same if we had an umiak, we could cross," said my wife.

"We have no wood," said someone.

"We have no skins," said someone else, "and there are steep shores on this island, and the tide washes so high. Where shall we find driftwood?"

"But we have some skins of seal," I said, "and maybe we can get more. And the handles of our harpoons will be some wood, and maybe we can get more."

We began to search hard everywhere upon the shores, and the search took many days and we did not find much. But we found some driftwood buried in the sand. It was old and not too strong, but it was driftwood just the same. And we killed more seals, and my wife was careful when she skinned the seals. We found also some bones and we saved the bones, even those which were very small, and the time came and though we had only half enough I started to build the umiak. "There will never be enough wood to build this umiak," someone said. And then one would find more driftwood. And then I kept on to build more of the umiak until there was no more wood, and at last everyone said, "There will be no umiak." And for many days there was only half an umiak and no one knew what to do.

We had used all the bones of our kills, all the wood we could find and even the ivory snow knife for a part of a rib. And then one day I heard sounds from my wife and our children, and when I looked down they were on the shore and they were digging up sand. "The bones of a whale," they were yelling, "the bones of a whale."

The bones of a whale. I could not believe what I was hearing. The bones of a whale. And they were good bones, these bones of a whale, and they were big bones, and I finished the umiak. Then everyone came and we sat down around it, and we laughed. "It is a funny umiak," everyone said.

We lowered it down by the traces of the dogs (all tied in one) over the edge of the steep cliffs and we put it in the water, and someone said, "Now it looks more funny still." Some of us climbed in, but, even so, with few of us in it, it was shaking all over.

"It will never carry us," said my wife.

"No, never," said everyone,

"Yes," I said, "it will carry us." And I said to my wife, "Get me a roll of your good sealskin line, and the bladders of the seals I told you to save." All around the umiak I fastened the line. And then I blew up the bladders of the seals and I tied them. And I fastened them to the sides, and then I said, "Now you who always doubt, get in."

And they got in, and my wife got in, and she said, "It will do, Comock, it will do."

And everyone said, "Ae, it will do."

Now we waited some days for no wind. But in these days, though the ice was all gone, with even a small wind there was always some sea. We waited more days, and now there were no more seals, and the eiders were gone, though there were still in the cliffs some sea pigeons. Upon these we lived. We waited more days, and on this day of today my wife said, "This is the smoothest of all our days on this island."

"Ae," I said, "we will wait, there is still enough sea."

But she said, "We should lower the umiak over the cliffs and all of us climb down and be ready to go." But I said, "No, we will wait until there is more smoothness come over the sea." But she said, "No, we will go"; and then I said, "No, we will wait until there is more smoothness come over the sea." But she said, "No we will go"; and then I said, "No"; then she said, "Yes"; then I said, "No." Then she went off and sat by herself, still like a stone.

Suddenly there were yells: "Umiak! Umiak!" And when I stood up there it was, your white sail going around the nose of the cape. And though there was not too much smoothness on the sea, we lowered our umiak over the cliffs and we put it in the water and we all got in.

And my wife said, "I have here in my hands a stick, and if anyone moves they will feel this stick, for there is not too much smoothness on the sea." And all the way she kept good watch with her stick.

"And now," concluded Comock, "we have come over to you on the sea, and you have taken us on your boat, and here we are."

"Ae," said his wife.

"Ae," said Comock, his wonderful face alight. "Ae, and now there are no more words in my mouth. Tiamak," he said.

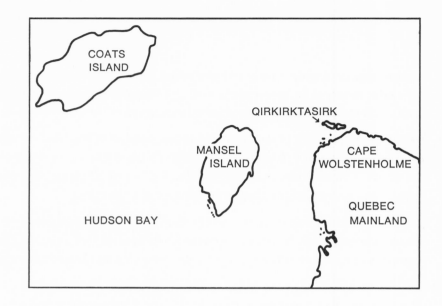

LATER EVENTS

The land which Comock described as leaning over the sea must have been
Cape Wolstenholme, and the island which rose straight up from the sea,
Qirkirktasirk Island where a colony of murres or sea birds can still be found.
As in the story, a strong current separates Qirkirktasirk from the mainland.
We will never be certain, but it is likely that the big island where Comock
spent ten years was Mansel Island, sixty miles west of Cape Wolstenholme.
On the north end of this island, a whaling wreck is still visible.

Mansel Island ranges from great glistening cliffs to flatlands that roll away, mile after empty mile, featureless and undifferentiated, save for quiet inland pools that reflect the sky's monotonous expanse.

Between the passing of one winter and the coming of the next, temperate, even warm weather prevails. Snow melts. Flowers bloom. Birds flock from the south. The land becomes somber brown — not colorless, but dead in color, save for the bright orange of lichen-covered rocks.

In the fall, shifting fog hovers over the dark, glistening beaches. In the winter, drifting snow blows out a person's footprints like candle flames. Temperatures reach fifty degrees below zero. Winds exceed seventy miles an hour.

The landscape conveys an impression of absolute permanence and detachment. It is not hostile. It is simply there — untouched, silent, complete. It is very lonely, yet the absence of all human traces gives you the feeling you understand this land and can take your place in it. Because the scene is so unlike anything one has met before, it tends to fall into abstract patterns: triangles of blue shadows on a field of white; surfaces puckered up like a quilt; sea-sky-snow, all a continuous curve. It is extremely beautiful and would be equally effective upside down.

To Comock's family, Mansel Island was a favored place. It provided enough seal and walrus, bear and caribou, to satisfy all their needs. To anyone but an Eskimo, however, it was barren, comfortless, desolate.

Shortly after Comock reached Cape Wolstenholme, the *N. T. Gifford,* a whaling vessel, burned off Qirkirktasirk Island. A survivor reached Coats Island, which adjoins Mansel. He built an igloo of stones and found old harpoons with which he hunted. But he lacked Comock's knowledge, and in the end was unable either to escape or survive.

Of Comock's later life, I have no certain knowledge. But an elderly Eskimo named Mangiuq, living at Ivugivik, near Cape Wolstenholme, says his father traveled by sled to Mansel Island and lived there for years with his family. Government records list Mangiuq as born on Mansel Island in 1907. He says his father went there because he liked daring adventures and because one of his brothers was a hunted murderer. His father was a fine-looking Eskimo, small but strong, and with a nose like Comock's. His father's name was Qumaq. It may just be a coincidence. The two stories differ on a number of points, but human truth is what contradicts itself most in time, and on all important points there is agreement. I think Qumaq was Comock. If so, his line survives and multiplies. Qumaq ("Louse") and his wife Mitiaqyuk ("Little Eider Duck") had thirty-five grandchildren and many great-grandchildren.

— Edmund Carpenter

When Robert Flaherty (1889–1951) was twelve, he accompanied his geologist father into the Canadian bush where he lived with Indians and fur traders. Later, as a mining engineer, he crossed the unmapped Ungava Peninsula twice, rediscovered islands lost since the time of Henry Hudson, and became the most prominent name in Canadian subarctic exploration. His love for the Eskimos was the scientist's love of subject: nothing but the truth would satisfy. When he made a film about them in 1922, he filmed everyday people doing everyday things, being themselves. Nanook of the North *is still being shown throughout the world.*

When Edmund Carpenter (1922–　) was thirteen, he went on the first of many expeditions that took him to the Pacific, Asia, Borneo, Siberia, and, particularly, the Canadian Arctic. He excavated ruins, studied the languages of the people with whom he lived, and filmed their dances and art. He is the author of Eskimo *and the editor of a collection of Eskimo poems entitled* Anerca.